Additional Photography
Gene (Pin) Moule

"My total dedication and obsession
with photography has taken me on
journeys into many remarkable areas
throughout Australia.
I captured much of this collection of
images using a specialist panoramic
camera. Because of the wider field
of view, this format enables me to
portray the true spirit of Australia on
film. Upon viewing these images
I am sure you will share with me the
tranquillity and solitude I experienced
whilst exploring the stunning beauty
of this country."

PETER LIK PUBLISHING

Telephone: 1300 364 391

CAIRNS
PO Box 2529 Cairns Queensland 4870 Australia
Telephone: (07) 4053 9000   **Fax:** (07) 4032 1277
sales@peterlik.com.au

peterlik.com

© **Peter Lik Publishing** BK27
ISBN 187658530 7

Front cover - The docklands precinct reflected in the waters of Port Philip Bay.
Back cover - Colours of Australia. The Twelve Apostles on the Great Ocean Road.
Front Cover Photograph - James Lauritz - courtesy of Tourism Victoria.
Other Photography - Courtesy of Tourism Victoria, Grant Campain.

MELBOURNE

AUSTRALIA

PETER LIK

Melbourne - the Cultural Centre of Australia

Proud host to the 2006 Commonwealth Games, Melbourne is one of Australia's most vibrant and cosmopolitan cities. A unique mix of traditional and contemporary architecture, and a casual European styling with a distinctive Australian flavour gives the city a character all its own.

Within the easy to navigate city grid is a network of hidden side streets and alleyways, where eclectic boutiques and cafes nestle comfortably between iconic world-class fashion houses. Historic landmark buildings and monuments seamlessly blend into a mosaic of well-tended parks and gardens woven into the city centre. The striking sharp edges of Federation Square, and the glittering opulence of Crown Casino blend harmoniously with painstakingly restored nineteenth century façades such as Flinders Street Station. The constant rumbling of Melbourne's famous tram system not only adds an old-world charm but is also the perfect way to discover the sprawling city's many attractions.

Melbourne's prolific culinary offerings are nothing short of legendary with a seemingly endless supply of cafes, restaurants and al fresco eateries. Home to an extraordinarily diverse multicultural population, the city is a dedicated foodie's delight. In the world famous Lygon Street precinct, every variation on the food theme imaginable abounds, while over in quirky beachside St Kilda, Acland Street's cakes and gourmet sweets offer a mouth-watering extravaganza. Virtually every nation of the world is represented somewhere in the city's melting pot of gastronomic choice.

Victoria's compact geography, and the city's close proximity to the picturesque attractions of the Great Ocean Road, the Dandenong Ranges and the wine-growing region of the Yarra Valley, makes Melbourne ideal for a short visit or an exciting destination to explore at length.

A city of beauty - an ever-evolving skyline, lush parklands, the Yarra River and the legendary Melbourne Cricket Ground.

Overleaf: The Crown Casino Fire-Towers light up the night sky along Southbank.

Left & Above: A perfect Melbourne day along the banks of the Yarra River.

Opposite: An age old meeting place, under the famous Flinders Street Station clocks.

A wondrous architectural fusion of steel, glass and stone, Federation Square on the banks of the Yarra.

Inner sanctuary,
St. Patrick's Cathedral.

The Gothic splendour of
St. Paul's Cathedral.

Overleaf: A kaleidoscope of colour,
Brighton Beach's famous bathing
boxes.

Left: Cook's Cottage, Fitzroy Gardens.

Above: The Royal Exhibition Building.

Opposite: A game of Australian Rules Football always draws a huge crowd to the hallowed Melbourne Cricket Ground.

The eternal flame at the Shrine of Remembrance is a tribute to fallen soldiers. Shrine Reserve Gardens.

Sculptured steelwork along the Citylink Tollway.

Ferries on the Yarra.

Giant tree ferns emerge from the mist of the Dandenong Ranges.

Yarra Valley & Dandenong Ranges

One of Australia's most spectacular natural regions lies just an hour from the centre of Melbourne. Protected by mountain ranges, the Yarra Valley's temperate climate offers ideal grape growing conditions and some of the world's finest wines are produced in its vineyards and wineries. Food, wine and tourism are the mainstays and the locals' legendary hospitality can play host to a day trip of wine tasting at the cellar door, or a more romantic weekend escape to one of many luxury boutique cottages.

Australia's oldest steam engine – the Puffing Billy – threads its way through the spectacular fern gullies and towering forests of the Dandenong Ranges offering a unique nineteenth-century view of the area. Renowned as an artistic mecca, the Dandenong's are dotted with quaint, authentic studios and teahouses to savour the local arts crafts and produce. For the more energetic, over 300 kms of walking tracks wind through the National Park, from which to experience first hand the thousands of species of native flora and fauna.

Above: Picturesque Yarra Valley wine district.

Shafts of sunlight warm the cool fern gullies of Sherbrook Forest.

Opposite Page: Timeless journey aboard Puffing Billy steam train in the Dandenong Ranges.

Overleaf: The fruit of the vine. Vineyard in the Yarra Valley.

The knobbies, craggy nesting ground of the little penguins.

Previous page: A magical fern gully. Sherbrook Forest in the Dandenong Ranges.

Phillip Island

The nightly spectacle of the famous Penguin Parade on Phillip Island attracts over half a million visitors annually, making it Australia's number one wildlife tourist destination. These tiny tuxedoed fellows waddle ashore every evening returning to their sand burrows after a day's fishing, oblivious to the hundreds of curious human onlookers. Unlike their larger counterparts, the appropriately named 'Little Penguin' sports a deep blue plumage for camouflage and is the world's smallest species, growing to only around 33cm tall.

Above: Little penguins arrive for their nightly ritual.

Overleaf: Wilson's Promontory.

Mornington Peninsula

Summer playground. Mt. Martha Beach.

An hour's drive from Melbourne, situated on the two bays of Port Phillip and Western Port, the spectacular Mornington Peninsula is almost completely surrounded by sea. Its boot shaped geography offers a glorious coastline with stunning beaches and a thriving holiday atmosphere. Reminiscent of the Mediterranean, tiny fishing villages stud the promontory and the larger towns of Portsea and Sorrento are a hive of aquatic activity. These picturesque coastal vistas, along with secluded hinterland hideaways and vineyards make the Mornington Peninsula one of the most popular recreational areas in Victoria.

View of Portsea Beach.

A reflection of autumnal beauty in country Omeo.

Opposite page: A colonial farmhouse afloat in a sea of lavender.

Mysterious Hanging Rock.

Opposite page: Monolithic masterpiece at the Grampian Ranges.

Above: The Australian Centre of Contemporary Art.

Left: The historic Shot Tower, the centrepiece of Melbourne Central.

Great Ocean Road

Stretching over 400 kms from Geelong in South Western Victoria all the way to the South Australian border, the Great Ocean Road has garnered the reputation as one of the world's most scenic drives. Along the length of its breathtaking coastline are such landmarks as the incredible natural rock formations of the Twelve Apostles, and the stunning Otway Ranges Rainforest. The area also boasts some of the best surf beaches in the world, including Bells Beach at Torquay, home to the internationally renowned classic surf tournament.

Previous page: Colours of Australia. The Twelve Apostles on the Great Ocean Road.

Natural haven. Hopetoun Falls in the Otway Ranges.

The Great Ocean Road winds its way along Victoria's rugged south-western coastline.

Lochard Gorge, rich in maritime history, Great Ocean Road.

The cityscape viewed from the historic fishing village of Williamstown.

Previous spread: The Docklands precinct reflected in the waters of Port Phillip Bay.

The historic St. Kilda Pier.

Luna Park, St. Kilda.

A bustling city backdrop contrasts with the seaside ambience of Brighton Beach.

Brilliantly lit fountains along the casino walk.

Above: The Princess Theatre is a landmark Melbourne building dating back to 1886. It is one of the city's many unique cultural assets.

Right: Dining out on Lygon Street.

Skyline viewed from Melbourne's tallest tower, the Rialto building, looking east to the Dandenong Ranges.

Peter Lik Galleries

Lik's original design concept was to create a contemporary space that enhances the natural beauty of his imagery, and the galleries continue to evolve under his direction. Attracting a diverse mix of visitors and collectors, the galleries are a fitting environment in which to experience an extraordinary photographic collection.

Each gallery offers the highest level of framing professionalism available and fully insures each piece, delivered to your doorstep worldwide.

A team of experienced Art Consultants are on hand to guide the visitor through their journey, or they can simply relax and enjoy the gallery at their leisure.

CAIRNS
4 Shields Street
Cairns Qld 4870 Australia
Telephone [07] 4031 8177
cairns@peterlik.com.au

LAHAINA
712 Front Street
Maui, Hawaii 96761 USA
Telephone [808] 661 6623
lahaina@peterlik.com

LAS VEGAS
Forum Shops at Caesars
3500 Las Vegas Blvd South
Las Vegas NV 89109 USA
Telephone [702] 836 3310
lasvegas@peterlik.com

NOOSA
Shop 2, Seahaven 9 Hastings Street
Noosa Heads Qld 4567 Australia
Telephone [07] 5474 8233
noosa@peterlik.com.au

PORT DOUGLAS
19 Macrossan Street
Port Douglas Qld 4871 Australia
Telephone [07] 4099 6050
port@peterlik.com.au

SYDNEY
Level 2 QVB
455 George Street Sydney
NSW 2000 Australia
Telephone [02] 9269 0182
sydney@peterlik.com.au

peterlik.com

Peter Lik - The Photographer

Peter Lik is one of the world's most innovative and prolific landscape photographers. His passion and dedication to his craft are unsurpassed, and Peter is recognised as the leader in his field.

He was born in Melbourne Australia in 1959, the only son of Czech immigrant parents. Completely self taught, Peter's talent for photography was evident from an early age. He first picked up a camera at the age of eight, and has retained a spirit and enthusiasm for his work that is equalled only by his unbounded energy and deep affinity for the land. It was whilst travelling in Alaska in 1994 that Peter's fascination with photography took a dramatic turn. Previously only working with 35mm cameras, he discovered the encompassing view of the panoramic camera and he was converted. It opened up a whole new world of creative possibilities and took him to another level in his photography.

In 1997 Peter took the courageous step of entering the competitive world of publishing with the birth of Peter Lik Publishing. He began with specialised panoramic postcards and the range of small hard cover books that have become his trademark. His first large format coffee table book "Australia – Images of a Timeless Land" is a stunning showcase of Peter's most emotive images. Now in its fourth reprint, the book received the prestigious "Galley Award" for excellence in production. Peter's latest publications are the magnificent "Spirit of America" and "Maui - Hawaiian Paradise."

The success of his publishing company provided Peter with the platform to fulfil a lifelong dream of opening his own galleries selling limited editions of his work. He opened his first gallery in his hometown of Cairns and due to an overwhelming demand, it was followed almost immediately by a second in Port Douglas.

Now with further galleries in Sydney, Noosa, Hawaii and Las Vegas, Peter Lik has established a credible presence worldwide. With handcrafted local timber floors and unique custom designed furniture, his galleries radiate a beautiful ambience and are a fitting environment in which to profile his work.

Peter's artistic landscapes have been recognised with a growing list of awards. The Australian Institute of Professional Photography (AIPP) has honoured his talents with their highest accolades. As an investment opportunity, Peter's images are increasing in value as respect and recognition for his work spreads throughout the world.